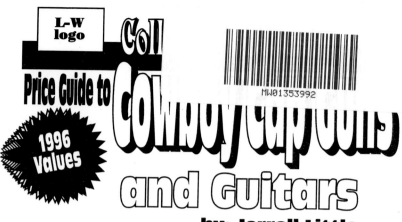

Price Guide to Collecting Cowboy Cap Guns and Guitars
1996 Values
by: Jerrell Little

Published by:
L-W Book Sales

© 1996
Jerrell Little

ISBN#: 0-89538-047-1

Copyright 1996 by Jerrell Little
L-W Book Sales

All rights reserved. No part of this work may be reproduced or used in any forms or by any means - graphic, electronic, or mechanical, including photocopying or storage and retrieval systems - without written permission from the copyright holder.

Published by: L-W Book Sales
P.O. Box 69
Gas City, IN 46933

Printed by IMAGE GRAPHICS, INC., Paducah, Kentucky

Please write for our free catalog.

Table of Contents

Dedication/Pricing Info............ 4	Cowgirl Cap Guns & Holsters 44-45
About The Author 5	Misc. Cowboy Collectibles 46-55
My Heroes and Their Horses 6	Autographed Photos 56-57
Cap Guns & Double Holsters...... 7-30	Guitars 58-88
Cap Guns & Single Holsters 31-36	Guitar Case 85-86
Cap Guns 37-43	Headstocks 87

Index

.44 Caliber Pistol 11, 37
Air Rifle 51
Autry, Gene 7-9, 11, 31, 35,
.... 37-38, 52, 56, 58-65
BB Pistol 36
Bonanza 15
Bronco 14, 30
Buffalo Bill 12
Buzz-Henry 8, 9, 38
Colt 45 39
Colt Texan 21
Crockett, Davy 16
Daisy Mfg....................... 36
Derringer 39
Fanner...................... 15, 33
George Schmidt Manufacturing 28
Gunsmoke/Matt Dillon 12, 16
Harmony Guitar 71
Hopalong Cassidy 15, 39
Hubley Manufacturing 10, 12, 14, 16,
.... 18-26, 29, 33-34, 36, 39-45, 57
Jones, Buck 51, 74
Kenton Mfg....................... 31
Kilgore Manufacturing 14, 30, 53
Kincaid, Bradley 83

Leslie-Henry 7-10, 13, 16, 31, 35,
.... 37-38, 40-41, 56
Lone Ranger............. 57, 68, 69, 70
Marx 50
Mattel................... 15, 32-33, 39
Maverick 14
Nichols Stallion 17-18, 27, 32, 46
Old Kraftsman 80, 82
Paladin Colt 45 36
Pioneer Days Guitar 79
Plainsman Guitar 75-76
Range Rider 28
RC Cola 16
Regal....................... 77-78
Rogers, Roy .. 7, 10, 38, 40, 53, 56, 66-67
Shooting Gallery 50
Silvertone Guitar 65
Singing Cowboy 71-73
Stallion .38 17-18
Stevens Manufacturing 40, 43
Supertone 58-61, 73, 83
Texan 14, 22-24, 29, 35, 44, 47, 57
Texan Jr..... 12, 16, 19-20, 22, 33, 41-43
Texas Ranger 21
Wild Bill Hickok 13, 41
Wyandotte 15, 39

Dedication

Thanks to my wife Carolyn, our son Jeff and his wife Sharon, and our son Tracy, who have helped tremendously with the research and preparation of this book.

Pricing Information

The values in this book should be used only as a guide. These prices will vary from one secion of the country to the other. All prices are also affected by the condition as well as the demand of the toy, etc.

Photo Credit: Trace Man Photography
113 Stoney Brook Drive
Lenoir, NC 28645

About the Author

Jerrell Little, a native of the North Carolina mountains, was born in Jefferson, NC and has lived in Boone, NC for the past 33 years.

Jerrell reminisces about going to the Parkway Theatre as a young boy, every Saturday to see his cowboy heroes. Ticket price was 9¢ while popcorn, drink, or candy was 5¢ each.

In his younger days he played music with several bands in the area and by the age of 15, he had his own band. Jerrell opened his own music store when he was 21, thus his interest in various musical instruments.

Jerrell started collecting antique guns at a very early age and has been a collector of various things ever since. Just a few of his favorite collectibles are: guns, bicycles, watches, toys, trains, musical instruments and most recently to satisfy his second childhood, cowboy guitars, cap guns and holsters.

He now lives in Boone with his wife, Carolyn. They have two grown sons, Jeff and Tracy. Jeff is an aspiring musician in Nashville and Tracy is a corporate credit manager for a manufacturing company and shares his Dad's interest in cap guns and holsters.

Jerrell still enjoys making music on occasion and travels to trade shows, flea markets and yard sales. But much to his disappointment, cap guns and holsters, which he used to buy for $5 or $10 have increased greatly in price as you can see in this book.

Look, reminisce and enjoy.

My Heroes and their Horses Names

COWBOYS	HORSES
Hoppy	Topper
Roy Rogers	Trigger
Dale Evans	Buttermilk
Gene Autry	Champion
Johnny Mack Brown	Blackjack
Allan Rocky Lane	Feather
Don Red Berry	Cyclone
Buck Jones	Silver
Tim McCoy	Hero
Sunset Carson	Silver
Bob Livingston	Shamrock
Rex Allen	Koko
Tom Mix	Tony
Lone Ranger	Silver
Tonto	Scout
Tim Holt	
Charles Starret	
Ken Maynard	
Bob Steel	
Tex Ritter	
Lash LaRue	
Whip Wilson	

Cap Guns & Double Holsters

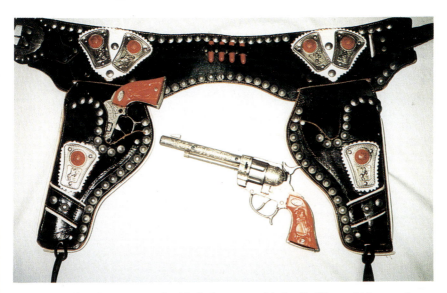

A 1950s Gene Autry double holster set with Leslie-Henry 11" guns that have revolving cylinders and red grips, manufactured by Leslie-Henry. The black holsters have red jewels and lots of studs.

      Good: $500   **Excellent: $650**   **Mint in box: $900**

A 1950s Roy Rogers gun and double holster set, the guns are manufactured by Leslie-Henry. The holster is made of heavy tooled leather with "Roy Rogers" done in silver under the bullets on the belt.

      Good: $500   **Excellent: $650**   **Mint in box: $1000**

Cap Guns & Double Holsters

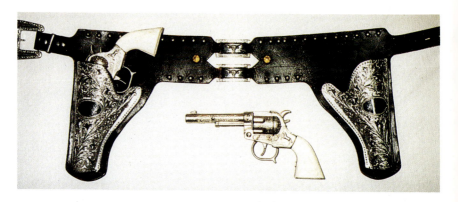

A 1950s Gene Autry double holster set with guns. The guns were manufactured by Buzz-Henry and are 7 1/2" with full grips, and a black holster trimmed with silver metal.

Good: $450   Excellent: $600   Mint in box: $800

A 1950s Gene Autry gold double holster set with guns that are manufactured by Leslie-Henry, and are 9" long. The holster is black with gold foil.

Good: $400   Excellent: $550   Mint in box: $700

Cap Guns & Double Holsters

A 1950s Gene Autry bronze double holster set with 9" long guns manufactured by Leslie-Henry. The belt is light brown with metal holsters.

Good: $550   Excellent: $700   Mint in box: $900

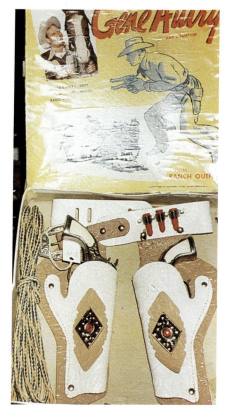

A 1950s Gene Autry double holster set with 7½" guns manufactured by Buzz-Henry. The belt and holsters are white trimmed in beige with red gems on holsters, in original box.

**Good: $300   Excellent: $400
Mint in box: $600**

Cap Guns & Double Holsters

A 1940s Roy Rogers double holster set with 8" cast iron cowboy guns that are manufactured by Hubley. The holster and belt is black, trimmed in white with red gem studs on belt.

        Good: $300   **Excellent: $400**   **Mint in box: $500**

A 1950s Roy Rogers set with two 9" gold Leslie-Henry guns that are very heavy. They are in a double holster with cuffs and spurs, (very heavy tooled leather). This is a copy of the double holster set that Roy Rogers wore in the movies. (There are many studs on the holster and cuffs with the initials "RR" on them.)

        Good: $600   **Excellent: $850**   **Mint in box: $1200**

Cap Guns & Double Holsters

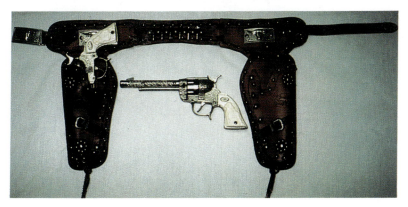

A 1950s Gene Autry double holster set with two .44 caliber pistols. The leather belt and holsters have lots of studs, and in the above close up picture you can see the Gene Autry signature, also marked "Flying A Ranch" on the holsters.

Good: $500 Excellent: $750 Mint in box: $1000

Cap Guns & Double Holsters

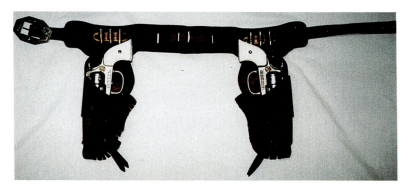

A 1940s Buffalo Bill holster set with Hubley cast iron "Cowboy" guns. The belt and holsters are brown and black leather.
Good: $175   Excellent: $250   Mint in box: $400

A 1950s Gunsmoke holster set with Hubley Texan Jr. guns. The leather holsters read Matt Dillon.
Good: $150   Excellent: $200   Mint in box: $300

Cap Guns & Double Holsters

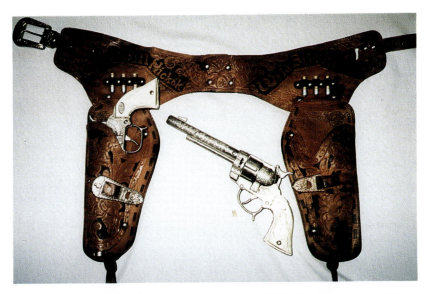

A 1950s Wild Bill Hickok holster and two 11" Leslie-Henry guns. (Very detailed leather with silver buckles).

Good: $450   Excellent: $600   Mint in box: $775

A 1950s Wild Bill Hickok holster and two 11" Leslie-Henry guns. The holster is red and tan leather (very heavy set).

Good: $375   Excellent: $450   Mint in box: $600

Cap Guns & Double Holsters

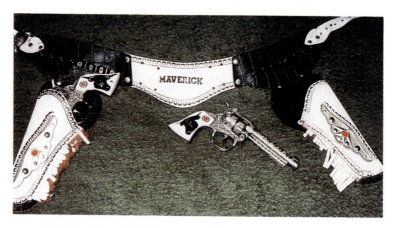

A 1950s Maverick holster set, with two Hubley Texan guns. The belt and holsters are done in black and white leather, with silver on the holsters.

Good: $125   Excellent: $175   Mint in box: $250

A 1950s Broncos holster set with two guns manufactured by Kilgore. Made of black leather with aluminum horses on the holsters where they fit onto the belt.

Good: $175   Excellent: $225   Mint in box: $350

Cap Guns & Double Holsters

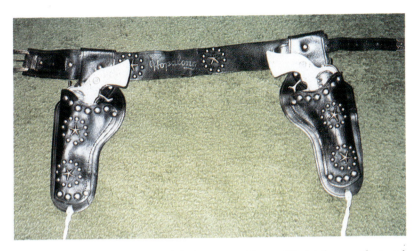

A 1950s Hopalong Cassidy holster set with two 9" pistols manufactured by Wyandotte.

Good: $600   **Excellent: $800**   **Mint in box: $1000**

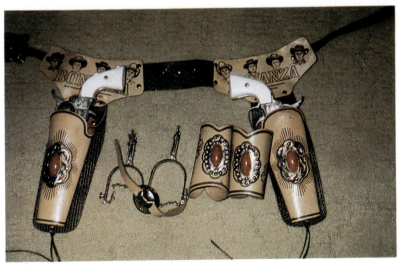

A 1960s Bonanza holster set with Fanner 50 guns, cuffs and spurs. The guns are manufactured by Mattel.

Good: $250   **Excellent: $350**   **Mint in box: $500**

Cap Guns & Double Holsters

A 1950s Davy Crockett holster with two Texan Jr. guns that are manufactured by Hubley.

Good: $250   Excellent: $300   Mint in box: $400

A 1950s RC Cola Matt Dillon Gunsmoke holster set with a Leslie-Henry pistol.

Good: $400   Excellent: $500   Mint in box: $700

Cap Guns & Double Holsters

A 1950s Stallion .38 holster set made of brown lizard like leather, manufactured by Nichols.

Good: $150   Excellent: $200   Mint in box: $300

A 1950s Stallion .38 holster set, manufactured by Nichols. The holsters look as if they are black leather but they are really made of rubber.

Good: $200   Excellent: $275   Mint in box: $350

Cap Guns & Double Holsters

A 1950s Stallion .38 holster set, black belt and holster with silver studs and red jewels. Manufactured by Nichols.
    Good: $175   **Excellent: $250**   **Mint in box: $400**

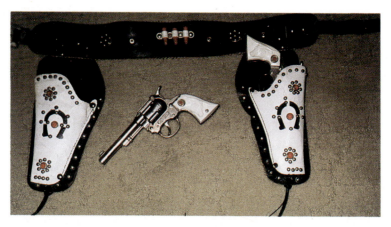

A 1950s Western holster set, manufactured by Hubley. The belt is black and the holsters are black and white with a horseshoe on each one and red jewels and lots of silver studs.
    Good: $125   **Excellent: $150**   **Mint in box: $225**

Cap Guns & Double Holsters

A 1950s Western holster set with Hubley pistols, the belt is light brown with grey (leather/cloth) covered holsters.
Good: $125   Excellent: $175   Mint in box: $250

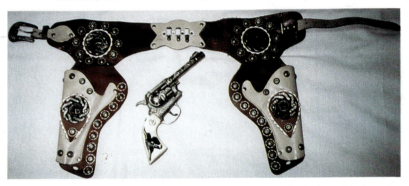

A late 1950s holster set with a Texan Jr. pistol. The belt and holster is done in brown and white with lots of studs.
Good: $150   Excellent: $225   Mint in box: $300

A 1950s Texan Jr. holster set in tan leather with red jewels, manufactured by Hubley.
Good: $125   Excellent: $175   Mint in box: $250

Cap Guns & Double Holsters

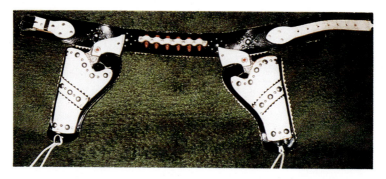

A 1950s Texan Jr. holster set, manufactured by Hubley. The belt and holsters are made of black and white leather with lots of studs.
Good: $125   **Excellent: $175**   **Mint in box: $250**

A 1950s Texan Jr. holster set, the guns have unusual turquoise grips, manufactured by Hubley.
Good: $150   **Excellent: $200**   **Mint in box: $275**

Cap Guns & Double Holsters

A 1950s Texas Ranger holster set with Hubley Western guns. The belt and holsters are in black and white with yellow jewels on them, and marked on the holster is "Texas Ranger".
    Good: $125   **Excellent: $175**   **Mint in box: $250**

A late 1930s Texan cast iron Colt Texan holster set, manufactured by Hubley. The holsters are furry with trim and have horses standing in the middle of horseshoes, done in metal.
    Good: $400   **Excellent: $550**   **Mint in box: $750**

Cap Guns & Double Holsters

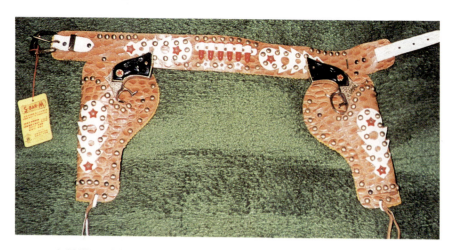

A 1950s gold Texan Jr. holster set, the guns were manufactured by Hubley, and the holster is by S-Bar-M Holsters. The leather belt and holsters have lots of gold studs all over.

Good: $200   Excellent: $300   Mint in box: $450

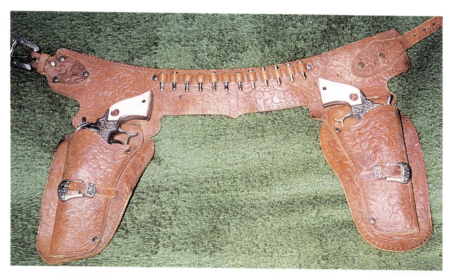

A 1940s Texan holster with Hubley cast iron Texan guns. The holster is heavy tooled leather, and the guns have a "Colt" logo in the grips. (This set is hard to find.)

Good: $400   Excellent: $500   Mint in box: $650

Cap Guns & Double Holsters

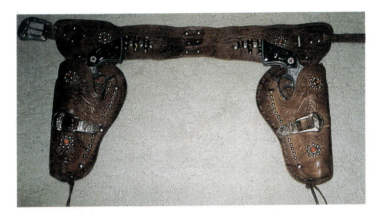

A 1950s Texan holster set, fancy tooled brown leather with studs and small red jewels, manufactured by Hubley. The Texan guns are satin finish die cast with black grips.
Good: $275   Excellent: $375   Mint in box: $550

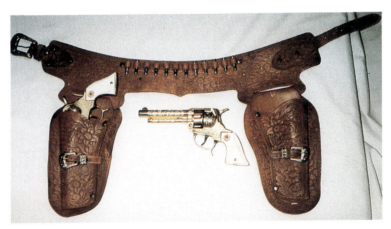

A 1950s Texan holster set, with diecast gold Texan pistols and a heavy tooled leather belt and holsters.
Good: $250   Excellent: $350   Mint in box: $500

Cap Guns & Double Holsters

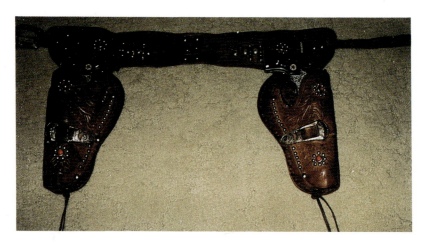

A 1950s Texan holster set with 9" Hubley Texan guns that have black grips. The holster is of heavy tooled leather.

Good: $300   Excellent: $400   Mint in box: $550

A 1950s cowboy holster set, with Hubley pistols. The belt and holsters are extremely heavy and fancy with lots of jewels and studs.

Good: $275   Excellent: $350   Mint in box: $500

Cap Guns & Double Holsters

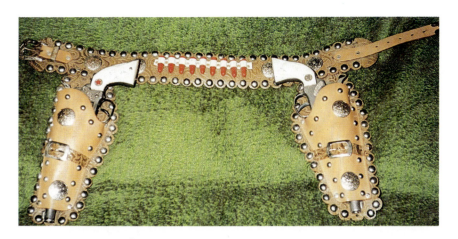

A 1950s Cowboy holster set, manufactured by Hubley. The holster is large and tan with lots of studs.
Good: $275   Excellent: $350   Mint in box: $500

A 1950s Cowboy holster set, manufactured by Hubley. The holster is large with lots of studs and is black and tan in color. This is an extremely fancy and highly decorated double holster set.
Good: $350   Excellent: $450   Mint in box: $600

Cap Guns & Double Holsters

A 1950s Cowboy holster set, manufactured by Hubley, made of leather and with studs on the holsters.
Good: $250   Excellent: $325   Mint in box: $425

Several Holster & Cap Gun sets shown here.
for reference only

Cap Guns & Double Holsters

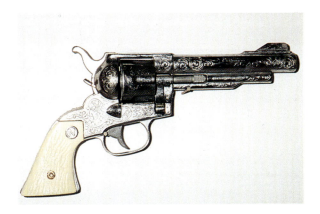

(closer view)

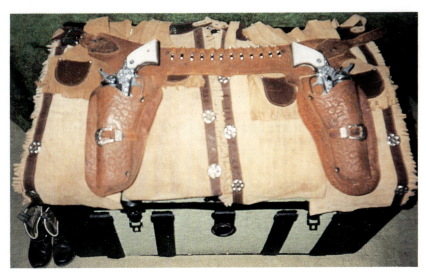

Early 1960s Nichols Stallion holster set with chaps 41-40. This set belongs to the Sons of the Author. He gave this set to them in the mid 1960s. They originally came with four guns, but only two survived all the gunfights. (These guns are rare.)

        Good: $500   **Excellent: $600**   **Mint in box: $750**

Cap Guns & Double Holsters

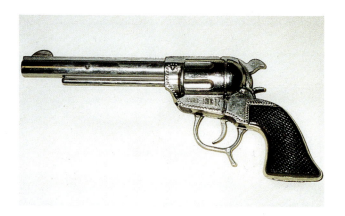

(closer view)

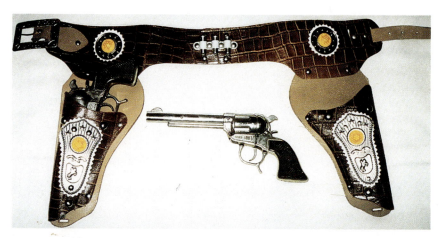

A late 1950s Range Rider holster set, manufactured by George Schmidt.
Good: $250   **Excellent: $350**   **Mint in box: $450**

Cap Guns & Double Holsters

(closer view)

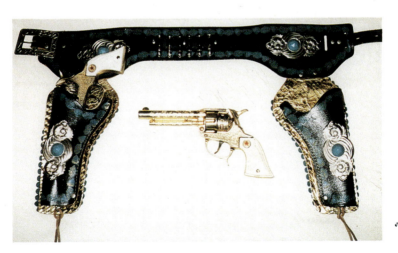

A 1950s Texan holster set with 9" guns, manufactured by Hubley.
Good: $350   Excellent: $450   Mint in box: $575

Cap Guns & Double Holsters

(closer view)

A 1950s Bronco holster set with guns, manufactured by Kilgore. This gun takes disc caps. (Jerrell Little had this set since early childhood).
Good: $200   Excellent: $250   Mint in box: $325

Cap Guns & Single Holsters

Two late 1930s early 1940s Gene Autry single holsters with cast iron guns, manufactured by Kenton.

Black holster set with bronze plated gun
Good: $300   Excellent: $400   Mint in box: $600

Tan holster with nickle plated gun
Good: $225   Excellent: $350   Mint in box: $450

A 1950s Gene Autry sheriff set with an 11" gun and a black holster and belt, badge, handcuffs, and pouch. Manufactured by Leslie-Henry, with Gene Autry's signature on the holster.

Good: $300   Excellent: $450   Mint in box: $600

Cap Guns & Single Holsters

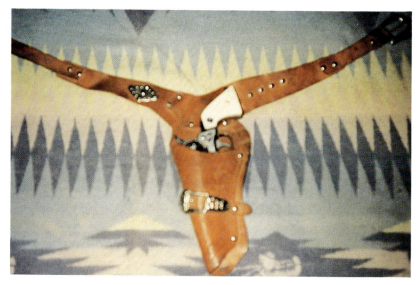

A 1950s early 60s, Nichols Stallion .38 caliber gun and single holster set.
Good: $75   Excellent: $100   Mint in box: $175

A 1960 single holster and .45 caliber gun that shoots shells, manufactured by Mattel.
Good: $125   Excellent: $175   Mint in box: $250

Cap Guns & Single Holsters

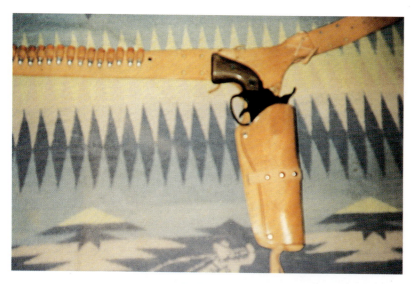

An early 1960s Fanner 50 single holster, manufactured by Mattel.
Good: $75 **Excellent: $125** **Mint in box: $175**

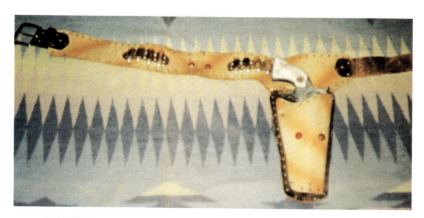

A 1950 Texan Jr. single holster and gun set manufactured by Hubley.
Good: $75 **Excellent: $125** **Mint in box: $175**

Cap Guns & Single Holsters

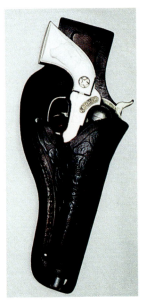

A 1950 Cowboy very thick brown leather single holster set. The gun is manufactured by Hubley.
**Good: $125   Excellent: $175
Mint in box: $250**

A 1950 Cowboy single, heavy leather tooled holster, with a Hubley made gun. (Missing the belt).
**Good: $150
Excellent: $225
Mint in box: $350**

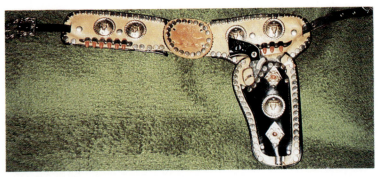

A 1950s Cowboy single holster and gun set in tan and black with lots of fancy studs and silver, manufactured by Hubley.
Good: $175   Excellent: $250   Mint in box: $325

Cap Guns & Single Holsters

A 1950s Gene Autry 9" gun and single holster set. The gun is manufactured by Leslie-Henry.
Good: $250   **Excellent: $325**   **Mint in box: $425**

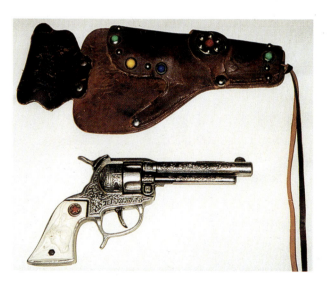

A 1940s single holster and a cast iron Texan gun.
Good: $150   **Excellent: $200**   **Mint in box: $250**

Cap Guns & Single Holsters

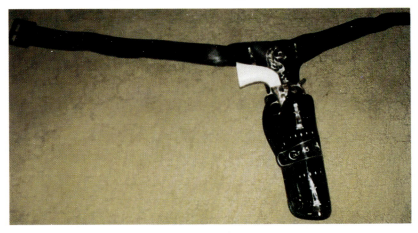

A 1960s Paladin Colt 45 single holster set, the gun was manufactured by Hubley.

Good: $225   Excellent: $275   Mint in box: $375

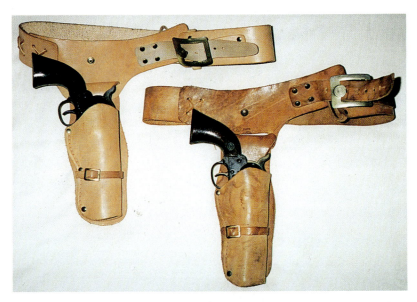

Two 1960s BB Pistols and single holster sets, manufactured by Daisy. These two sets belong to the author's sons and were given to them in the early to mid 1960s.

Good: $75 each   Excellent: $125 each   Mint in box: $200 each

Cap Guns

A 1950s Gene Autry .44 caliber gun, manufactured by Leslie-Henry, 11" long, with a full red grip.
Good: $100
Excellent: $175
Mint in box: $275

A 1950s Gene Autry gold gun, manufactured by Leslie-Henry, 9" long.
Good: $100
Excellent: $150
Mint in box: $250

A 1950s Gene Autry .44 caliber pistol, manufactured by Leslie-Henry, 11" long. (This gun takes bullets), rare.
Good: $125
Excellent: $175
Mint in box: $325

Cap Guns

A 1950s Gene Autry gun, manufactured by Leslie-Henry, 9" long.
Good: $100
Excellent: $150
Mint in box: $250

A 1950s Gene Autry gun, manufactured by Buzz-Henry, 7 1/2" long with a full white grip.
Good: $65
Excellent: $125
Mint in box: $200

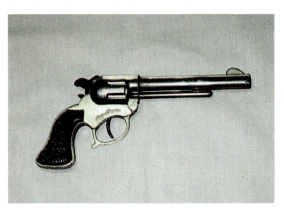

A 1950s Roy Rogers gun, 8 1/2" long, very rare.
Good: $200
Excellent: $275
Mint in box: $350

Cap Guns

A 1950s Hopalong Cassidy gun, manufactured by Wyandotte with Hopalong's signature below a picture of him on the grip of the gun.
Good: $200
Excellent: $300
Mint in box: $600

A 1950s Colt 45, manufactured by Hubley, with a revolving cylinder and bullets.
Good: $100   Excellent: $150   Mint in box: $225

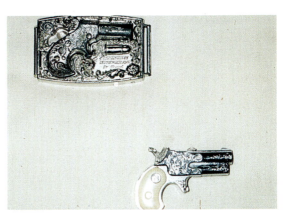

A 1950s and a 1960s shooting shell belt buckle derringer, manufactured by Mattel.
The other is a Nichol Derringer.
Mattel Derringer
Good: $50   Ex: $75
Mint in box: $125
Nichols Derringer
Good: $20   Ex: $30
Mint in box: $50

Cap Guns

A 1940s Sheriff, cast iron pistol, manufactured by Stevens.
Good: $75
Excellent: $125
Mint in box: $200

A 1940s Cowboy cast iron gun, manufactured by Hubley.
Good: $75
Excellent: $125
Mint in box: $175

A 1950s Roy Rogers gun, manufactured by Leslie-Henry, 9" long.
Good: $125
Excellent: $175
Mint in box: $350

Cap Guns

A 1950s Wild Bill Hickok, 11" Leslie-Henry pistol.
Good: $100   Excellent: $175
Mint in box: $250

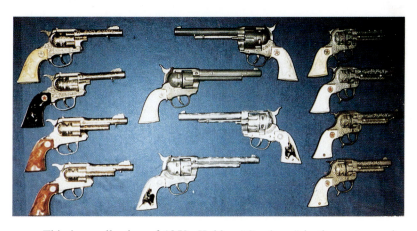

This is a collection of 1950s Hubley "Cowboys" in the center, and different Texan Jr. variations on the left and right sides.

Texan Jrs.
Good: $40-60   Excellent: $60-80   Mint in box: $150-200

Cowboys
(pictured in the middle row)
Good: $75-100   Excellent: $100-150   Mint in box: $250

Cap Guns

A 1950s Texan Jr. pistol with the original box, by Hubley.
Mint in box: $200

A late 1950s Texan Jr. cap pistol with the original box, by Hubley.
Mint in box: $150

Cap Guns

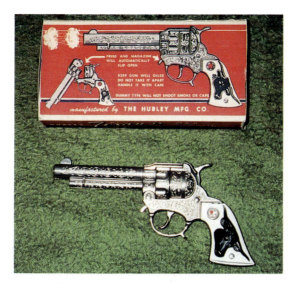

A Texan Jr. pistol with the original box, manufactured by Hubley.
Mint in box: $200

A 1940s Sheriff's set which includes a cast iron pistol, a badge, and children handcuffs, manufactured by Stevens.
(for reference only)

Cowgirl Cap Guns & Holsters

(closer view)

A 1940s-1950s white cowgirl set, including double holsters, cast iron Texan guns, matching cuffs, spurs, and a rifle. The guns were manufactured by Hubley. (Notice the holsters are reversed on the belt, this is an extremely nice set.)

    Good: $500   **Excellent: $650**   **Mint in box: $800**

Cowgirl Cap Guns & Holsters

(closer view)
These guns are marked "Cowboy" but belong to this cowgirl set.

A 1950s white cowgirls set, including double holsters with lots of jewels and studs. The guns are manufactured by Hubley. (This set was won as a door prize at a department store at a Christmas drawing in the mid 1950s.)
Good: $400   Excellent: $600   Mint in box: $800

Miscellaneous Cowboy Collectibles

Pony Saddle and Double Holster set.
(for reference only)

A handmade Stagecoach and horses with two Nichols Stallion 41-40 guns.
(for reference only)

Miscellaneous Cowboy Collectibles

This Texan double holster set with chaps and vest belongs to the author's sons. They were given to them in the early to mid 1960s. The guns were made of cast iron and were Colt Texans.
(for reference only)

Miscellaneous Cowboy Collectibles

Cowboy Boots
(for reference only)

A wooden toy pistol and gun rack, made in the 1950s.
(for reference only)

Miscellaneous Cowboy Collectibles

Boxes of caps used through the 1930s to the 1950s. **(for reference only)**

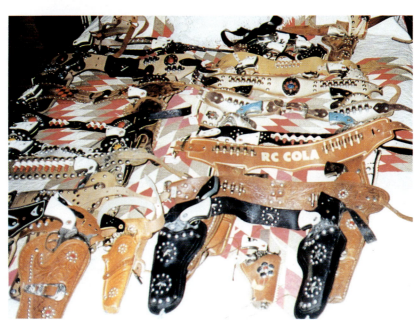

A collection of double holster sets. **(for reference only)**

Miscellaneous Cowboy Collectibles

1950s Knockdown Target Shooting Gallery and original box, by Marx, with a double barrel shotgun that shoots darts at the targets.
Good: $75   Excellent: $150   Mint in box: $250

Miscellaneous Cowboy Collectibles

A 1930s to 1940s Buck Jones air rifle, cap gun with holster, and guitar.

BB Gun – Good: $200   Excellent: $250   Mint in box: $300
Holster only – Good: $125   Excellent: $200   Mint in box: $300

Miscellaneous Cowboy Collectibles

Pictured is a Gene Autry Guitar, a metal sign, a holster with a Leslie-Henry pistol, and a watch. **(for reference only)**

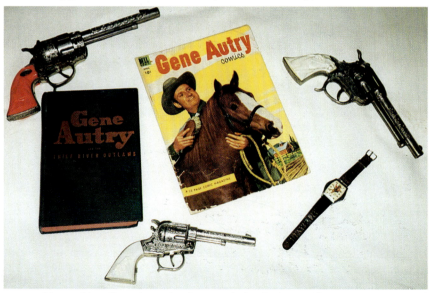

Pictured is a Gene Autry book, a comic book, three different Leslie-Henry pistols, and a watch. **(for reference only)**

Miscellaneous Cowboy Collectibles

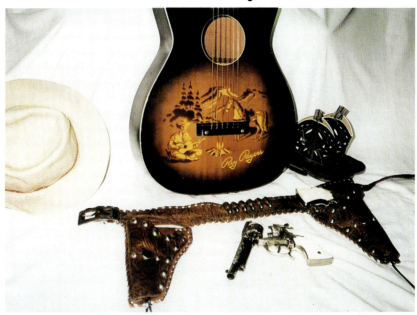

Pictured is a Roy Rogers guitar, a double holster, guns, boots, and a cowboy hat. **(for reference only)**

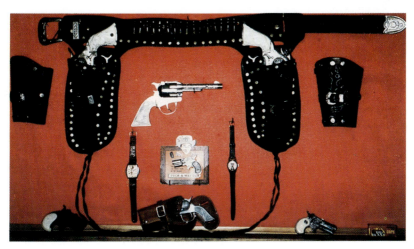

Pictured is a Roy Rogers double holster set, cuffs, tuck-a-way gun, a Kilgore 8 1/4" gun, and a small gun holster.
(for reference only)

Miscellaneous Cowboy Collectibles

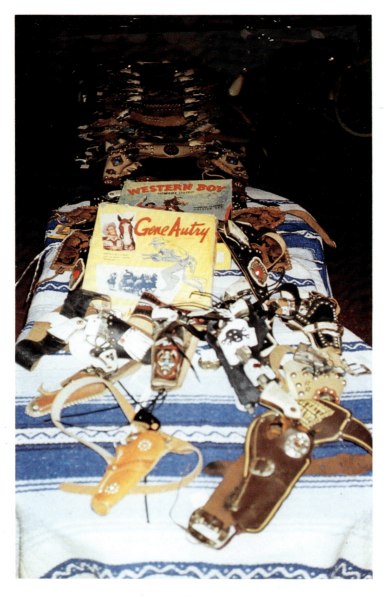

A collection of holsters and guns.
(for reference only)

Miscellaneous Cowboy Collectibles

A collection of Western Guns
(for reference only)

A collection of double holster sets
(for reference only)

Autographed Photos of Cowboys & Their Cap Guns

An autographed picture of Gene Autry with a Leslie-Henry Gene Autry cap pistol.

(for reference only)

An autographed picture of Roy Rogers with a Leslie-Henry 9" pistol.
(for reference only)

Lone Ranger Autographed Photo and Comic Books/Cap Guns

The Lone Ranger autographed picture and two different comic books. One is "The Lone Ranger" the other is "The Lone Rangers Famous Horse Hi-Yo Silver", both are by Dell.
(for reference only)

A 1950s Lone Ranger single holster and an 8" pistol, manufactured by Hubley Texan.

Good: $175   Excellent: $250   Mint in box: $325

Guitars

A 1933 Gene Autry guitar, manufactured by Supertone. These first models of Gene Autry guitars say "Roundup" on the headstock. It has a 13" wide body and a 12 fret neck. The cowboy scene is done in red stencil, on a brown guitar.

Good: $300   Excellent: $450

Guitars

An early 1930s Gene Autry guitar, manufactured by Supertone, the headstock says "Roundup", and has a 13" wide body and a 12 fret neck. The cowboy scene is done in brown and tan stencil, on a brown guitar, and has a Gene Autry signature at the bottom of the scene.
Good: $300   Excellent: $450

Guitars

A 1932 Gene Autry guitar, manufactured by Supertone, the headstock says "Roundup", and has a 14" wide body and a 14 fret neck. The cowboy scene is done in brown and tan stencil, on a brown guitar, and has a Gene Autry signature at the bottom of the scene.

Good: $300   Excellent: $450

Guitars

A 1936 Gene Autry guitar, manufactured by Supertone, the headstock says "Old Santa Fe". This is a hard to find brown "archtop guitar". This was also the largest Gene Autry guitar made with a 15" wide body and a 14 fret neck and has a Gene Autry signature at the bottom.

Good: $400   Excellent: $600

Guitars

A 1946 Gene Autry guitar, sold by Sears, Roebuck and Company. The cowboy scene is done in red and yellow stencil, on a brown guitar, and has a Gene Autry signature at the bottom of the scene.

Good: $250   Excellent: $350

Guitars

A 1950s Gene Autry guitar, sold by Sears, Roebuck and Company. The cowboy scene is done in red and yellow stencil, on a brown guitar, and has a Gene Autry signature at the bottom of the scene.

Good: $250   **Excellent: $350**

Guitars

A 1939 Gene Autry guitar, grand concert size, sold by Sears Roebuck and Company. The signature of Gene Autry goes up the neck, and this guitar has a slotted headstock. This sold in a 1939 Sears catalog for $9.98, and now it is very hard to find.

Good: $400   Excellent: $500

Guitars

A late 1950s Gene Autry guitar, sold by Sears Roebuck and Company, the headstock says "Silvertone". This was the last of the cowboy type stencil guitars made. The cowboy scene is done in red and white stencil, on a red guitar.

Good: $150   Excellent: $225

Guitars

A 1950s Roy Rogers guitar, sold by Sears, Roebuck and Company, that has his signature along with his picture on the headstock. It has a 13" wide body and a 12 fret neck and is 36" long. The singing cowboy scene is done in yellow and brown stencil with a Roy Rogers signature at the bottom all done on a dark brown guitar.

Good: $250   Excellent: $350

Guitars

A 1950s Roy Rogers guitar, sold by Sears Roebuck and Company, with his picture and signature on the headstock. It has an 11" wide body and a 12 fret neck and is 33" long. On the inside of the guitar it reads "Roy Rogers Enterprises". This one is harder to find than the bigger size guitar. The singing cowboy scene is done in yellow and brown stencil with a Roy Rogers signature at the bottom all done on a dark brown guitar.

Good: $275   Excellent: $375

Guitars

A 1930s Lone Ranger guitar, sold by Sears Roebuck and Company. This model has a high gloss finish and a different pattern on the neck, and the headstock is plain. The scene is of the Lone Ranger and Tonto on their horses and is done in orange-red and off-white stencil that reads "Hi-Ho Silver! The Lone Ranger".

Good: $300   Excellent: $450

Guitars

A 1930s Lone Ranger guitar, sold by Sears Roebuck and Company. The headstock says "Lone Ranger". The scene is of the Lone Ranger and Tonto on their horses and is done in orange-red and off-white stencil and reads "Hi-Ho Silver! The Lone Ranger".

Good: $225   Excellent: $375

Guitars

A 1930s Lone Ranger guitar, sold by Sears Roebuck and Company, and has a Lone Ranger signature on the headstock. (This version reads "Hi-Yo Silver" instead of Hi-Ho Silver) with the scene of the Lone Ranger and Tonto on their horses done in red and silver stencil on a black guitar. This guitar sold in the 1939 Sears catalog for $6.75.
Good: $225   Excellent: $375

Guitars

A 1930s and 1940s Singing Cowboys guitar, sold by Sears Roebuck and Company, that says "Harmony" on the headstock. This guitar sold for $4.25 in 1939. The scene of the cowboys are in red and yellow stencil, and the top of the guitar says "Singing Cowboys" in red. The guitar is a brown sunburst color.

Good: $175   Excellent: $300

Guitars

A 1930s Singing Cowboy guitar, sold by Sears Roebuck and Company. The scene of the cowboys singing around a camp fire is in red and yellow stencil, and the top of the guitar reads "Singing Cowboys" in red. The guitar has a gun metal color finish, (or grey).
Good: $225   Excellent: $350

Guitars

A 1930s Singing Cowboy guitar, sold by Sears Roebuck and Company, and has a sticker inside the guitar that reads "Supertone". The scene of the cowboys singing around a camp fire is in red and yellow stencil, on a black finished guitar.

Good: $175   Excellent: $300

Guitars

An early 1940s Buck Jones guitar, sold by Montgomery Ward. The scene is of Buck sitting on his horse with the signature that reads "Good Luck Buck Jones/Silver", that is done in black and white stencil, on a medium brown guitar.

Good: $275   Excellent: $400

Guitars

A late 1930s early 1940s Plainsman guitar, sold by Montgomery Ward. The scene has a cowboy on his horse beside a tree, the headstock reads "The Plainsman". It has a 14" wide body and is 37" long overall. The scene is in black and white stencil, on a green finished guitar.

Good: $275   Excellent: $400

Guitars

A late 1930s early 1940s Plainsman guitar, sold by Montgomery Ward. The scene has a cowboy on his horse beside a tree, the headstock reads "The Plainsman". It has an 11 1/2" wide body and is 32" long overall. This version is harder to find than the larger one. The scene is done in green and brown stencil, on a bronze colored guitar.

Good: $300   Excellent: $425

Guitars

A 1950s guitar, manufactured by Regal. The scene is of a big cowboy hat and a cowboy on a rearing horse, the headstock reads "Regal". It has a 13" wide body and is 37" long overall. The scene is done in white stencil, on a medium brown finished guitar.

Good: $250   Excellent: $350

Guitars

A 1950s guitar, manufactured by Regal. The scene is of a big cowboy hat and a cowboy on a rearing horse, the headstock reads "Regal". This guitar is harder to find than the brown ones. The scene is done in brown stencil, on a cream colored guitar.

Good: $275   Excellent: $375

Guitars

A 1950s guitar, with a scene of a wagon train across the prairie, the front of the guitar reads "Pioneer Days". The scene is done in tan stencil, on a medium brown guitar.

Good: $275   Excellent: $375

Guitars

A guitar, manufactured by Old Kraftsman, with a scene of some cowboys near a campfire and it reads "Old Kraftsman" on the headstock. The scene is done in white stencil, on a medium brown finished guitar.

Good: $200   **Excellent: $300**

Guitars

A guitar that has an unusual tail piece, with a scene of cowboys near a campfire. The scene is done in white stencil, on a dark brown finished guitar.

Good: $200   Excellent: $300

Guitars

A guitar, manufactured by Old Kraftsman, with a scene of some cowboys and a stage coach near a campfire, and it reads "Old Kraftsman" on the headstock. The scene is done in white stencil, on a dark brown finish with a light brown sunburst finish on the body. (Note the unusual finish on the neck of the guitar.)

Good: $200   Excellent: $300

Guitars

A 1930s Bradley Kincaid Houn'Dog guitar, manufactured by Supertone for Sears Roebuck and Company, with a slotted headstock. The scene is of a hound dog running and mountains in the background. The scene is a very colorful decal, on a light brown finished guitar.

Good: $300   Excellent: $500

Guitars

A black guitar with a slotted headstock, marked "Round up". (No other information is available at this time on this guitar.)

Good: $200   Excellent: $300

Guitars

A 1935 Gene Autry guitar with its original case, manufactured by Supertone.

Good: $225   Excellent: $350

Guitar Case

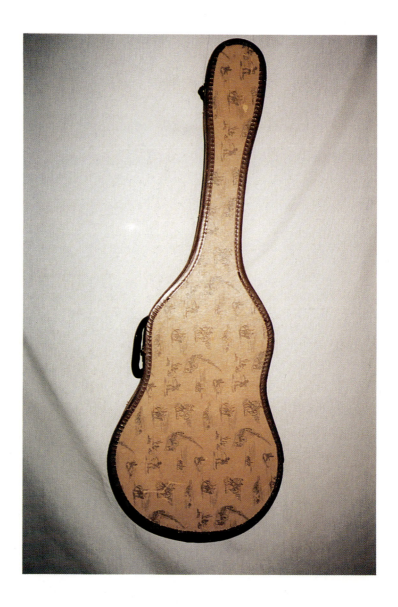

A 1950s guitar case with all different kinds of cowboy scenes. These cases are very hard to find.

Good: $50   Excellent: $100

Guitar Headstocks

Eleven different headstocks of cowboy guitars.
(for reference only)

Guitars

These are the three most popular styles of Gene Autry guitars from the 1930s, 40s and 50s.
The tan one is from the 1930s.
The brown one is from the 1940s.
The black one is from the 1950s.